For David ~ M.H.

For my family and friends ~ C.C.

VIKING
Published by the Penguin Group
Penguin Books USA Inc., 375 Hudson Street, New York, New York 10014, U.S.A.
Penguin Books Ltd, 27 Wrights Lane, London W8 5TZ, England
Penguin Books Australia Ltd, Ringwood, Victoria, Australia
Penguin Books Canada Ltd, 10 Alcorn Avenue, Toronto, Ontario, Canada M4V 3B2
Penguin Books (N.Z.) Ltd, 182–190 Wairau Road, Auckland 10, New Zealand

Penguin Books Ltd, Registered Offices: Harmondsworth, Middlesex, England

First published in Great Britain by Frances Lincoln Ltd., 1996

First published in the United States of America by Viking,
a division of Penguin Books USA Inc., 1996

1 3 5 7 9 10 8 6 4 2

Text copyright © Meredith Hooper, 1996
Illustrations copyright © Christopher Coady, 1996

Library of Congress Catalog Card Number: 95-61828
ISBN 0-670-86259-2

The author and artist would like to thank Dr. Wendy Kirk
of the Geology Department, University College London, and Dr. Angela Milner
of the Department of Palaeontology, The Natural History Museum, London, for their help.

Printed in Hong Kong
Set in Goudy Bold

THE PEBBLE IN MY POCKET

A History of Our Earth

MEREDITH HOOPER

Illustrated by CHRIS COADY

VIKING

At the back of the book is a geological timeline charting
the main periods in earth's history, from around
4.6 billion years ago to the present day. Animals not
named in the text are labeled on the timeline.

Although the story of The Pebble in My Pocket traces the way
a single pebble is formed, the animals illustrated come from
various locations and were chosen as typical of the
geological times in which they lived.

THE PEBBLE in my pocket is round and smooth and brown.
   I found it on the ground.
Where did you come from, pebble?

Under the volcano melted rock shifts like thick syrup. The molten rock is nine times hotter than boiling water.

The rocks covering the earth are cold and hard. They form a thin crust about 18 miles thick beneath the continents, but only three miles thick under the oceans. The deeper you go down inside the crust the hotter it gets. Below the crust lies mantle rock, so hot it can start creeping and shifting and melting.

The ground shakes. Gas hisses from the top of the volcano. Columns of purple ash shoot into the sky. Glowing fragments hurl through the air. Then the lava comes, molten rock spilling red-hot down the volcano's sides, and flowing out over the land.

The lava cools. It hardens, forming a thick wrinkled skin of new rock.

Everything is still. The seas swarm with living things. But nothing is living on this land.

It is 480 million years ago.

Slowly, very slowly, the surface of the earth begins rising. The rock made from the lava begins to tilt up, slowly, very slowly. All the rocks underneath go up. Everything that is on this piece of earth is rising. Huge slabs of rock tilt and twist. The land folds and buckles and crumples.

Two great landmasses, like giant plates, are colliding, pushing against each other, making mountains.

Every winter snow falls. Every summer the snow melts
and the sun shines on the rocks. Heat makes the rocks
expand. Cold makes them shrink. They expand and shrink,
expand and shrink. Then they crack.

Water seeps into cracks in the rocks. On cold nights
the water freezes. Clear crystals of ice push on the inside
of the cracks, wedging pieces of rock slowly apart.

Rain falls on the mountains and runs down the rocks.
Little leafless plants grow in damp places; they are some of
the first living things on the land.

It is 395 million years ago.

In the middle of summer, in the middle of the night, an enormous slice of cliff splits away from a mountainside and crashes down, shattering into fragments. Pieces of rock rumble and bounce down the mountain like a river of stone.

Rain falls on the new jagged edges of the rock, and the hot sun heats it, and the frost cools it. The wind blows, every day. Tiny specks of sand blow against the corners and edges of the rock, nibbling at their sharpness. Slowly, slowly, the sharp edges begin to be smoothed.

Everything on the surface of the earth is slowly being
eroded and broken down into smaller and smaller pieces.
Boulders powder into streaks of mud. Cliffs crumble to
grains of sand. The tops of mountains disintegrate into
pebbles. It has always happened. It will always happen.
It is happening now. All that is needed is time.
And the weather.

Wormlike creatures burrow in moss jungles,
and millipedes shelter under the rock.
    It is 390 million years ago.

The rain pours down, loosening the earth. Mud and rocks slide off the mountainside into a river. The river rushes along, dragging silt, sand, gravel, and boulders, stripping away the mountain's surface, layer by layer.

The river tumbles and rolls the rock, chipping edges, smoothing corners, rubbing it against other rocks. Gradually the rock becomes rounder, smaller. The river widens, flowing brown and slow.

The current nudges the rock past forests of ferns where spiders hide. It eases the rock through swamps where fish haul themselves out of the water and begin to breathe the air.

The rock travels for thousands and thousands of years. When it reaches the sea it is a smooth round brown pebble.

It is 375 million years ago.

Boulders and rocks embedded deep in the soil of the mountain look like permanent residents. They aren't. They are just passing through, like everything else, all on the way to the bottom of the sea.

The river drops the pebble onto a beach filled with other pebbles. The waves of the sea wash them backward and forward, grinding them up and grinding them down, rattling and clinking the pebbles together: striped pebbles, spotted pebbles, gray, brown, and white pebbles. Each pebble has come from its own special rock. Each was made in its own time and place.

Shiny grains of sand settle between the pebbles. The sand fills the spaces like the mixture between nuts in a brownie.

Slowly the sea starts to flood the land. The sea covers the pebbles packed in their grains of sand. Gradually the sand hardens, forming a new layer of rock, a conglomerate. The sea covers the cliffs and drowns the mouth of the river and washes into the forests.

It is 340 million years ago.

Creatures swarm and slither in the warm sea.
The tiny bodies of dead sea creatures drift down
onto the seabed, layer upon layer. Fine mud
drifts down, and sand. As each layer presses down,
the layers beneath slowly harden and the particles
cement together to form more rock, layers of
sedimentary rock under the sea.

The surface of the earth begins to rise, lifting the layers of rock to make new land above the water. Club-moss trees crowd in dank swamps and giant amphibians hunt among rotting wood and buzzing insects. But the pebble is still buried deep under the ground, beneath layers of sandstone and mudstone and limestone.

It is 300 million years ago.

The surface of the earth continues rising. It goes up more than three feet every two thousand years. The layers of sandstone and limestone, mudstone and conglomerate which were once under the sea are pushed up and up. They tilt and fold and crack. In 10 million years they have risen 16,000 feet, and now there are seashells and the fossils of dead sea creatures on top of mountains.

Dry winds blow sand from distant deserts. The layers of rock wear away, as they always do. And in some places the rock with the pebbles stuck in it begins to show through. It starts splitting and breaking into slabs.

A slab tumbles down a cliff.

A reptile with leathery wings and a long thin tail glides onto
the slab. A dinosaur with legs as big as tree trunks treads on the
slab and cracks a lump off.

It is 155 million years ago.

At night small mammals scurry across the lump of rock while the dinosaurs sleep. In the day they crouch under the rock while the dinosaurs hunt.

Gradually the mixture holding the pebbles together crumbles into grains of sand. The pebble is released.

It is 67 million years ago.

A meat-eating dinosaur attacks a plant-eating dinosaur. In the fight the pebble skids into a river. The pebble settles on a sandbar, with dinosaur bones and driftwood, drowned moths and flowers, because now there are flowers in this land.

It is 65 million years ago.

The river flows in a new course, and the pebble lies buried in the old riverbed. The dinosaurs have long since died out. Now, grass grows, and herds of long-legged animals graze above the pebble. A furry, two-horned rodent pushes past the pebble in its burrow.

It is 15 million years ago.

The wind blows colder and colder. Snow falls. Blizzards blot out the light. The snow packs down layer on layer. Deep underneath the surface snow, the old snow turns into clear blue glacier ice.

The glacier starts shifting, moving slowly downhill, grinding forward, a monstrous river of ice scraping across the land, scouring out valleys, sculpting mountains. The glacier picks up and moves everything in its way. It picks up the pebble and freezes it deep in its icy blue depths.

The glacier grinds on for thousands and thousands of years, roaring and groaning as the ice slides and shifts. Its surface is split with shadowy crevasses.

Gradually the weather begins to warm, and the glacier begins to melt. The ice releases its grip. Boulders, rocks, pebbles, sand, gravel, all are dropped on the ground, mixed together in great jumbled heaps. Old rocks, young rocks, rocks made under the sea and rocks formed under the crust of the earth, rocks from close by and rocks from far away, all lie on top of each other.

Everything has been moved from where it used to be.

Mammoths lumber past. A baby mammoth treads on the pebble, pushing it deep into the heap of stones.

It is a million years ago.

Floods leave the pebble high on a riverbank. People come to fish and hunt and build shelters. They stand on the pebble and sleep on it and drop grease from half-cooked lumps of meat.

In the night a rat creeps in, sniffing for food. A boy picks up the pebble to throw at the rat. He misses. The pebble rolls under a bush and down a hole.

It is 200,000 years ago.

The cold comes back. People move away. Massive ice sheets cover the land, burying forests and meadows. When warmth returns the melting ice drops the pebble in a lake. It sinks into the soft mud, while hippos wallow above in the warm water.

It is 125,000 years ago.

A new glacier gouges the pebble out of the bottom of the lake and pushes it, clasped in its clear blue depths, for thousands and thousands of years. Then the ice retreats, leaving the pebble on the slope of a valley.

Shaggy bison graze the long grass. New people come, hunting for food. Saber-toothed tigers watch. They can hunt what they like.

It is 12,000 years ago.

The pebble hasn't moved much since the last ice age.

It has been kicked and trodden on by animals and people. Cattle have grazed over it. Farmers have grown crops on it. A new road runs near it. Houses are built next to the road, and their foundations cover rocks and earth, pebbles and gravel.

But the houses miss the pebble. It lies, smooth and warm, in the sun.

The pebble in my pocket is round and smooth and brown. I found it on the ground.

My pebble has been on top of mountains and under the sea. It has been buried in ice and buried in rock. It has been covered in drying sand and tropical forest. It has been flung and dropped, frozen, soaked and baked, squeezed and squashed. It has been stood on and sheltered under and used. It has traveled huge distances, over immense periods of time.

My pebble is 480 million years old. So far.
Keep traveling, pebble!

Every pebble in the world is different from every other pebble.
Every pebble has its own story. Pick up a pebble and you are holding
a little piece of the history of our planet.

When did it all happen?

The story of *The Pebble in My Pocket* begins with a lava flow from an erupting volcano, 480 million years ago. Nine-tenths of earth's history has already happened. Geological changes occur over staggeringly huge periods of time. They are caused by constant tiny events, difficult to see—the action of water, wind, and sun, and the downward pull of gravity. They are everyday forces which happen every day. They have always happened, and they are happening right now.

Geologists divide the earth's history into various time periods. The chart on the right is a geological timeline, from the beginnings of the earth, around 4.6 billion years ago, to the present day. Some of the animals that appear in this book are shown below.

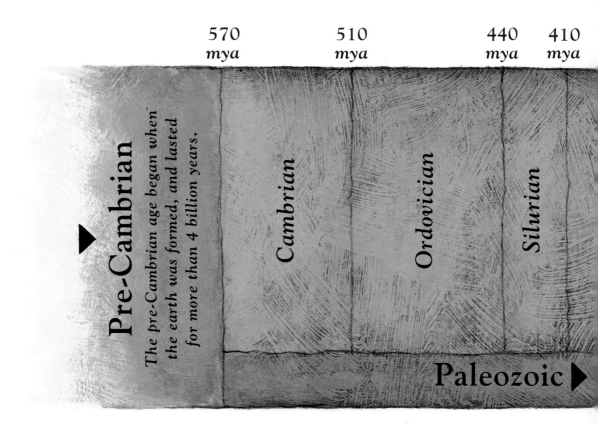

570 *mya*   510 *mya*   440 *mya*   410 *mya*

Pre-Cambrian

The pre-Cambrian age began when the earth was formed, and lasted for more than 4 billion years.

Cambrian

Ordovician

Silurian

Paleozoic ▶

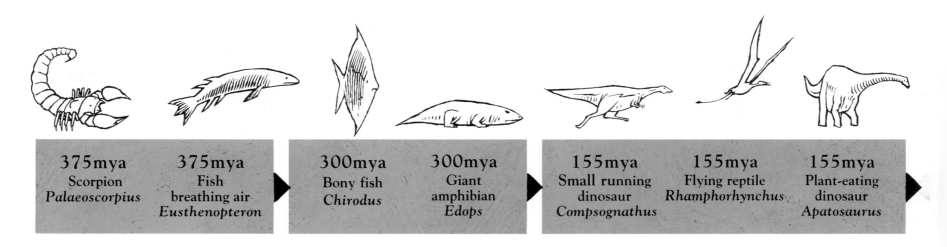

| 375mya Scorpion *Palaeoscorpius* | 375mya Fish breathing air *Eusthenopteron* | 300mya Bony fish *Chirodus* | 300mya Giant amphibian *Edops* | 155mya Small running dinosaur *Compsognathus* | 155mya Flying reptile *Rhamphorhynchus* | 155mya Plant-eating dinosaur *Apatosaurus* |

These pictures are not drawn to scale.

mya= million years ago

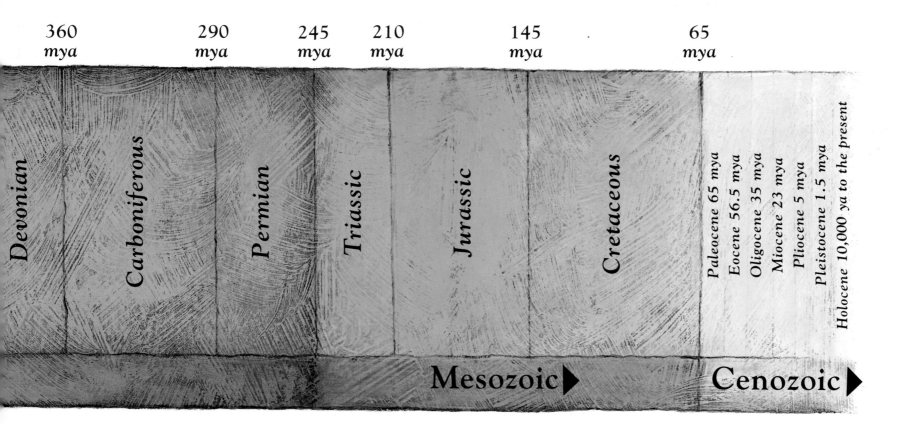

360
mya

290
mya

245
mya

210
mya

145
mya

65
mya

Devonian

Carboniferous

Permian

Triassic

Jurassic

Cretaceous

Paleocene 65 mya
Eocene 56.5 mya
Oligocene 35 mya
Miocene 23 mya
Pliocene 5 mya
Pleistocene 1.5 mya
Holocene 10,000 ya to the present

Mesozoic ▶

Cenozoic ▶

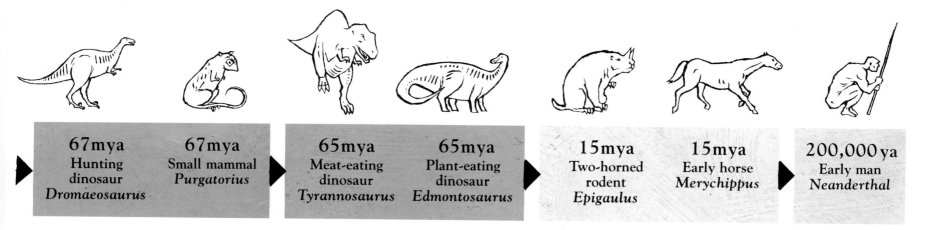

67mya
Hunting
dinosaur
Dromaeosaurus

67mya
Small mammal
Purgatorius

65mya
Meat-eating
dinosaur
Tyrannosaurus

65mya
Plant-eating
dinosaur
Edmontosaurus

15mya
Two-horned
rodent
Epigaulus

15mya
Early horse
Merychippus

200,000ya
Early man
Neanderthal